Akathist Hymn
to the
Holy Spirit

Pr. Sorin Benescu

Copyright © 2012 Pr. Sorin Benescu

ISBN: **978-606-30-1201-3**

DEDICATION

To His All-Holiness Ecumenical Patriarch
Bartholomew who blessed me,
also
to my father, John, who prays and whom
I owe a lot.

ACKNOWLEDGMENTS

Thanks to my wife, Dana,
for her help in correction and editing
and for the support without which the akathist
would not have seen the light of day,
also thanks to dr. Simona Carniciu for help in
correction.

PREPARATORY PRAYERS:

If you are a priest:

Glory to the Father, and to the Son, and to the Holy Spirit, both now and ever, and to the ages of ages. Amen.

If you are not a priest:

In the name of the Father and the Son and the
Holy Spirit. Amen.
Glory to You, our God, glory to You.
Heavenly King, Comforter, the Spirit of truth,
present everywhere and filling all things, Treasurer of Goodness and Giver of life, come and abide in us and cleanse us from every impurity, and save our souls, Gracious Lord.
Holy God, Holy Mighty, Holy Immortal, Have mercy on us.
Holy God, Holy Mighty, Holy Immortal, Have mercy on us.
Holy God, Holy Mighty, Holy Immortal, Have mercy on us.
Glory to the Father and the Son and the Holy
Spirit;

Both now and forever and to the ages of ages. Amen.
All-holy Trinity, have mercy on us.
Lord, be merciful to our sins.
Master, forgive our transgressions.
Holy One, visit us and heal our infirmities, for
Your name's sake.
Lord have mercy, Lord have mercy, Lord have mercy.
Glory to the Father and the Son and the Holy Spirit;
Both now and ever and to the ages of ages. Amen.

Our Father in Heaven,
hallowed be Your name,
Your kingdom come,
Your will be done on earth as it is in Heaven.
Give us this day our daily bread
and forgive us our sins,
as we forgive those who sin against us.
And lead us not into temptation,
but deliver us from evil.
For Yours is the Kingdom and the Power and the
Glory,
Father, Son and Holy Spirit,
now and forever and to the ages of ages. Amen.

The Creed
I believe in one God, the Father, the Almighty,
Creator of heaven and earth,
and of all things visible and invisible.
And in one Lord, Jesus Christ,
the only-begotten Son of God,
begotten of the Father before all ages,
light from light,
true God from true God,
begotten not created,
of one essence with the Father;
through whom all things were made.
For us and for our salvation

He came down from heaven,
and was incarnate of the Holy Spirit
and the Virgin Mary,
and became man,
and was crucified for us under Pontius Pilate,
and suffered and was buried,
and rose on the third day according to the
Scriptures,
and ascended into heaven,
and is seated at the right hand of the Father.
He will come again in glory
to judge the living and the dead,
and his kingdom will have no end.
And in the Holy Spirit,
the Lord, the Giver of Life,
Who proceeds from the Father,
Who together with the Father and the Son
is worshipped and glorified,
and Who spoke through the Prophets.
In one holy, catholic and apostolic Church.
I acknowledge one baptism for the forgiveness of sins.
I expect the resurrection of the dead,
and the life of the age to come. Amen.

KONTAKIONS AND OIKOSES:

Kontakion 1

O, Heavenly King, Holy Spirit, One before the ages, You Who sanctify all beings, both visible and invisible, glorious Lord, One of the Holy Trinity, in Whom every knee shall bow: those heavenly, those earthly and those underneath; because of this, as those who are enlightened by the Holy Baptism in Your name, the Father's and the Son's, the Thrice-holy. Although being unworthy, we dare to bring You this song of praise; and You, as He Who sanctifies and fulfills everything, our Comforter, hearken to the voice of the prayer of Thy servants and do not depart Your grace from us, because we always cry to You from the bottom of our souls: **Come, O Heavenly King, Comforter, and dwell in us and cleanse us from every impurity and save our souls, Gracious One!**

Oikos 1

Archangels and Angels, Virtues and Powers, Dominions and Principalities, standing before the throne of glory of the Holy Trinity, cannot herald the treasure of Your perfections. The many-eyed Cherubims and the Seraphims, those with six wings, covering their faces with fear and love, in You, O Joyful Light, talk to one another: Holy, Holy, Holy Lord of Sabaoth, for "*who is so great a God as our God? Thou art the God that doest wonders*"[1]. And being thankful and remembering, following the doxology of those in heaven with fear, faith and love, bowing our knees, we call You, O Most Holy Spirit, You, the One Who mysteriously identifies with us and still remains different, so we say such things as these:

Come, O Most Holy Spirit, The true Light, Whose glory is full of greatness,

Come, O Most Holy Spirit, the eternal Life and life-giving,

Come, O Most Holy Spirit, the hidden Mystery, Who art everywhere,

Come, O Most Holy Spirit, Treasure impossible to name, Who cleanse us from every stain,

Come, O Most Holy Spirit, ineffable Person, by Whom we confess Jesus Christ Son of God,

Come, O Most Holy Spirit, Person incomprehensible, Who pray for us with sighs too deep for words,

---

[1] *Ps.* 77.13,14.

Come, O Heavenly King, Comforter, and dwell in us and cleanse us from every impurity, and save our souls, Gracious One!

Kontakion 2

Speaking with the Lord and seeing the valley full of dry bones, Ezekiel has spoken: *Thus saith the Lord God; Come from the four winds, O breath, and breathe upon these slain, that they may live. So I prophesied as he commanded me, and the breath came into them, and they lived, and stood up upon their feet, an exceeding great army. Then he said unto me, Son of man, these bones are the whole house of Israel.*[2] So with fear and love, in deep wonder, we praise the Trinity, the Existing One, Father, Son and Holy Spirit, One God, and call upon Thee, Holy Spirit: O King, burn the thorns of the multitude of our sins with the fire of Thy divinity, thus letting us sing to God with pure heart: Alleluia!

Oikos 2

Seeking to understand the incomprehensible, Moses, the great among the prophets, said to the Father through Thee: *I beseech Thee, shew me Thy glory*! I hanker to know You, to see You as You are. But Father said to him: *I will put thee in a clift of the rock, and will cover thee with my hand while I pass by, thou canst not see my face: for there shall no man see me, and live.*[3] But to us, although being

---

[2]See *Ezekiel*. 37.1-14.

unworthy, the Father condescended to show Him in the image of His only-begotten Son, Who has sent Thou from the Father as cloven tongues like as of fire, at Pentecost, Thee, Who do not have image inward another divine Person but reveal Yourself in those deified, to sanctify us and through us the entire creation; for this, thanksgiving we say such things:

Come, O Most Holy Spirit, O God, sanctify us, the creation of the Holy Trinity, for Thy holy Name,

Come, O Most Holy Spirit, the Joy before ever of the Father and the Son,

Come, O Most Holy Spirit, Who own existence only from the Father and show the humility of the Son and rise His judgment,

Come, O Most Holy Spirit, Who proceed only from the Father, and Who affirm the Son,

Come, O Most Holy Spirit, Who proceed from the Father towards the Son, and shine from the Son to the Father,

Come, O Most Holy Spirit, Who are the Father's joy for the Son and the Son's joy for the Father[4],

Come, O Heavenly King, Comforter, and dwell in us and cleanse us from every impurity, and save our souls, Gracious One!

---

[3]Exodus 33.19-22, https://www.lds.org/scriptures/ot/ex/33?lang=eng, accessed on 4/6/2017.

[4]See pr. prof. dr. D. Stăniloaie, *Rugăciunea lui Iisus și experiența Duhului Sfânt*, Ed. Deisis, Sibiu, 2003, p. 110-128.

Kontakion 3

With Thy untold power, together with the Son and the Father, You keep all, administer them all, give life to all of them, rejoice them all. O the One in three suns, maker of all things, Holy Trinity, You measured the sky with your right hand, and the earth with the palm of your hand and through the Holy Spirit You support and revive all beings and call them all by their names. O Spirit the Most Holy, Who accomplish through the Son what the Father wants, there is no one that can hide from the strength of Your eyesight. On account of these, humbly obeying, together with all the Powers above and underneath, we sing to You: Alleluia!

Oikos 3

Having all creation serving the Holy Trinity, You reveal everywhere the signs of the Providence and of Your great perfections; Life flows through You; for this, cogitating, we see over all creatures the unseen works of Yours and the forever sanctifying power and the Godhead; for this, with wonder and joy, we call You, the Good Spirit of Holy Trinity's grace, Who guide us, and say like these:

Come, O Most Holy Spirit, You who survey everything, even the depths of God,

Come, O Most Holy Spirit, through Whom God reveals His secrets,

Come, O Most Holy Spirit, Who search the hearts and know the whole movements of thoughts,

Come, O Most Holy Spirit, Which moved *upon the face of the waters*, at the beginning, when *darkness was upon the face of the deep*,[5]

Come, O Most Holy Spirit, He Who *saith unto the churches; To him that overcometh will I give to eat of the tree of life, which is in the midst of the paradise of God*,[6]

Come, O Most Holy Spirit, He Who *saith unto the churches; He that overcometh shall not be hurt of the second death*,[7]

Come, O Heavenly King, Comforter, and dwell in us and cleanse us from every impurity, and save our souls, Gracious One!

Kontakion 4

Having inside the stormy heresy which ruined souls, the third Judah, fool Macedonius, followed by Maratoniu the deacon, estranged from You, denying Your being One of the Trinity; and although we confess the Hypostasis of the Father, another of the Son and another of Thy, the Holy Spirit, we testify with our hearts and with our lips one Godhead in the Father and in the Son and in Thee Holy Spirit, equal power, consubstantial glory; enlightened with the thrice illuminating light of the Holy Baptism's bath, we worship one God, singing to Thee, the Holy Spirit, and to the Father and to the Son: Alleluia!

---

[5] *Gen.* 1.2.

[6] *Revelation.* 2.7.

[7] *Revelation.* 2.11.

Oikos 4

As the pastors and the teachers of the holy Church heard that Macedonius entered the speaking herd of Christ like a terrible beast with foreign spirit and took away the sheeps from the true and righteous confession of faith, You gathered them in a synod at Constantinople; they confessed Thee as God and not as created thing and, honoring Thee along with the Father and the Son, prayed with wonderful voice:

Come, O Most Holy Spirit, Who bring the Son's joy to the Father,

Come, O Most Holy Spirit, in Whose light the Son shines,

Come, O Most Holy Spirit, Who get the same uncreated energy from the Father as the Son, but in Your own way,

Come, O Most Holy Spirit, Who possess all the divine essence in Your own way,

Come, O Most Holy Spirit, Who confirm the Father and the Son,

Come, O Most Holy Spirit, The completely invisible, not portrayed and untouched,

Come, O Heavenly King, Comforter, and dwell in us and cleanse us from every impurity, and save our souls, Gracious One!

Kontakion 5

Thank You, for You, God over all, have united with my soul in an unmelted, unmutated and unchanged way and revealed Yourself as the whole in all for me, an ineffable and unspent Food that overflows on the lips of my soul and gush in the spring of my heart, Vestment that flashes and burns the demons, Purification that cleanses myself through imperishable and holy tears which You gift to those that Thou approach; for this, in Your presence and through You we sing to God: Alleluia!

Oikos 5

We thank You for turning Yourself out in light without evening and in Sun that never sets, for there is no place to hide Thou Who fill all with Your glory. For You never hid from anyone but we are the ones who always hide from You, unwilling to come to You. For where would You hide Yourself, The One Who has no place to rest? Or why would You hide Yourself, You, the One Who never turns back from someone, nor turn anyone back? For this, bowing our knees, we call You:

Come, O Most Holy Spirit, You Who are both bursting fire and refreshing water,

Come, O Most Holy Spirit, The One Who burns and sweetens and makes corruption disappear,

Come, O Most Holy Spirit, Who turn men into gods and darkness into light,

Come, O Most Holy Spirit, Who remove mortals from hell and make them imperishable,

Come, O Most Holy Spirit, Who pull darkness towards light and keep the night in Your fist,

Come, O Most Holy Spirit, Who envelop the heart in light and transform us entirely,

Come, O Heavenly King, Comforter, and dwell in us and cleanse us from every impurity, and save our souls, Gracious One!

Kontakion 6

So now dwell Thee, O Lord, in us, live and remain unseparated in us, Thy servants, until the end, O Good, so that we find ourselves in Thee, O Good, when leaving the world and beyond our exit and reign with Thee, God over all. Remain, Lord, and do not leave us alone, being and living in us, so that when our enemies come, those who hunt our souls, they flee altogether and have no power against us, seeing You, the most powerful of all, sitting inside the home of our humble souls, which sing with You: Alleluia![8]

Oikos 6

Yes, Master, as You remembered us when we were in the world and in ignorance, and You chose us Yourself, separated us from the world and made us stand before Your glory; so now keep us safe sitting ever motionless inside Thy dwelling in us, so that we, the deads, constantly seeing You, be alive and say like these:

Come, O Most Holy Spirit, the endless Cheerfulness,
Come, O Most Holy Spirit, the Light without evening,

---

[8]See pr. prof. dr. D. Stăniloaie, *Rugăciunea lui Iisus și experiența Duhului Sfânt*, Ed. Deisis, Sibiu, 2003, p. 50.

Come, O Most Holy Spirit, the true Expectation of all those who want to be redeemed;

Come, O Most Holy Spirit, the Waking up for those who lie,

Come, O Most Holy Spirit, the Resurrection of the dead,

Come, O Most Holy Spirit, the Almighty Who constantly make and change all only by Your will,[9]

Come, O Heavenly King, Comforter, and dwell in us and cleanse us from every impurity, and save our souls, Gracious One!

Kontakion 7

Wanting to show to the fallen human race the great love and mercy of our God, the One glorified in Trinity, when the fullness of the time was come, Father sent his begotten Son, Who, being born of the Virgin, placed Himself under the law, to redeem those under law; spending on earth as a man and ransoming us by His cross, He ascended into heaven, where, fulfilling the promise, He sent You, Spirit of the Most Holy, the One Who shares the fullness godhead in a personal, unique manner, to men's hypostases inside the Church, to us all, to be able to sing: Alleluia!

Oikos 7

Wonderful indeed new miracle You pointed out, Marvelous One among the highest, when after Your coming over the chosen disciples and apostles, You accompanied them to preach all over the

---

[9]*Ibidem*, p. 49.

world, to proclaim the great name of the Holy Trinity and bring the Gentiles to the obedience of faith. For this, marveled at the power of their words and work, those inspired by Thee, joyfully we speak:

Come, O Most Holy Spirit, The One Who unites with humans and makes them sons of God,

Come, O Most Holy Spirit, The One Who burns us with the Divine longing and hurts us without sword,

Come, O Most Holy Spirit, The One Who endures, suffers and rewards not immediately,

Come, O Most Holy Spirit, The One Who is beyond everything and sees what everybody does,

Come, O Most Holy Spirit, The One Who is far from us, but sees everyone's facts,

Come, O Most Holy Spirit, Who give us patience not to be covered by sorrow[10],

Come, O Heavenly King, Comforter, and dwell in us and cleanse us from every impurity, and save our souls, Gracious One!

Kontakion 8

Once, at Mamre, Abraham saw You foreign, wonderful, the True God; and after years, You, the most gracious and totally transcendent Spirit, clothed his successor, the Most Pure Virgin and Holy Mary, with the dazzling and unapproachable brightness of Thy holiness, making her the Mother of the Word of God, Empress of the Angels, for our

---

[10]See diac. Ioan I. Ică jr., *Op. cit.*, p. 67.

salvation. For this, together with the Prophets and the Apostles, we sing to God through You, saying: Alleluia![11]

Oikos 8

Entire art everywhere, Thou the Holy Spirit, for always caring for all creation is the Trinity, with the strength of His immeasurable power which made everything. So having Thyself for us, we, the poor, actually drinking, eating and dressing in You every moment, we delight in unspeakable goodness, enriching forever with Your glory, we pray to You:

Come, O Most Holy Spirit, The One Who always stays unmoved and moves Himself entirely every hour and comes to us who lie in hell,

Come, O Most Holy Spirit, The One Who is above all the heavens, Holy and Most Holy,

Come, O Most Holy Spirit, the most desired and incessantly whispered Name, although it is totally forbidden to us to speak what You are or how You are or what way You are,

Come, O Most Holy Spirit, the everlasting Joy, Consolation of my humble soul,

Come, O Most Holy Spirit, the unfading Crown, my Breath and my Life,

Come, O Most Holy Spirit, Life-maker, Who proceed from the Father, worshiped and glorified together with the Son and the Father[12],

---

[11]See *Acatistier*, Ed. Arhiepiscopiei Sucevei si Rădăuţilor, p. 47.

[12]*Ibidem*, p. 49.

Come, O Heavenly King, Comforter, and dwell in us and cleanse us from every impurity, and save our souls, Gracious One!

Kontakion 9

All the creatures, up and down, unceasingly glorify God the Trinity One being, in You, The One Who scatter the storm of pagan gods; in heaven, some sing day and night: Holy, Holy, Holy; others put their crowns at the feet of the Godhead; and we, on earth, with all creation, being decorated by the face of Your glory, call Thee and also expect great and rich grace from Thee, because You are all the good, all the glory and all the delight and You deserve the glory together with the Father also with the Son, the One in essence and life-giving Holy Trinity, honored, known and adored by all faithful people and by Thee we sing to God: Alleluia![13]

Oikos 9

The saints have You, the Light of the world, and spend in light and they are enlightened, because You have dwelt in their hearts, O tremendous mystery, impossible to be described in human words or written by the hand, for the glory and the praise of the One beyond any word; for this, we call You so:[14]

---

[13]See *Acatistier*, Ed. Arhiepiscopiei Sucevei si Rădăuţilor, p. 49 şi Diac. Ioan I. Ică jr., *Op. cit.*, p. 51.
[14]See diac. Ioan I. Ică jr., *Op. cit.*, p. 52, 53.

Come, O Most Holy Spirit, in Whom the Trinity finds His perfection,

Come, O Most Holy Spirit, Who make us shine like sons, Comforter, sent by the Son from the Father,

Come, O Most Holy Spirit, Who give us the son's sensitivity and help our weakness,

Come, O Most Holy Spirit, You bring the light of God within us and move us and grant us the Grace of the Holy Trinity,

Come, O Most Holy Spirit, You bring the divine energy into creation, Treasurer of good things, Who fulfill all,

Come, O Most Holy Spirit, Who make impossible impersonal relationships between people, through Whom we all pray to the Father,[15]

Come, O Heavenly King, Comforter, and dwell in us and cleanse us from every impurity, and save our souls, Gracious One!

Kontakion 10

Wanting to save the world, the Most Holy and Divine Trinity shown Himself at Jordan River: the Father witnessed from heaven of His beloved Son; the Son, in the likeness of men, received the baptism from a servant; and Thou, O God, the Most Holy Spirit, descended like a dove over The One Who was baptized. So in the name of One God, but in three faces: the Father, the Son and the Holy Spirit, we learned to baptize and call upon Thee on every Chrismation of every man that cometh into

---

[15]See pr. prof. dr. D. Stăniloaie, *Op. cit.*, p. 110-128.

the world, singing: Alleluia!

Oikos 10

How would I describe, O Master, the view of the face of my Christ? How shall I say the view impossible to express of His beauty, revealed by Thee? How will comprehend the speech of my tongue the One Who is impossible to be included by the whole world? But, oh, high brightness light! Oh, motions of the fire! Oh, encircling of flames worked inside us, the very wicked, by Thee and Thy glory! And I know and I say that You are the Glory, the Most Holy Spirit of one essence and of one honor with the Word and with the Father, God over all! We worship Thee, we thank Thee and Thee call:[16]

Come, O Most Holy Spirit, Who help us to know those given to us by the good Lord,

Come, O Most Holy Spirit, the One Who shows us the love above all virtues,

Come, O Most Holy Spirit, Who overcome human wisdom and come powerfully,

Come, O Most Holy Spirit, the One Who says to the Churches: *To the one who is victorious, I will give some of the hidden manna. I will also give that person a white stone with a new name written on it, known only to the one who receives it.*[17]

Come, O Most Holy Spirit, the One Who says to the dead: *Blessed are the dead who die in the Lord from now on, they will rest from their labor,*

---

[16]See diac. Ioan I. Ică jr., *Op. cit.*, p. 160,161.
[17] *Rev.* 2.17.

for their deeds will follow them.[18]

Come, O Most Holy Spirit, the One Who says together with the bride: Come! *And let him that heareth say, Come. And let him that is athirst come. And whosoever will, let him take the water of life freely,*[19]

Come, O Heavenly King, Comforter, and dwell in us and cleanse us from every impurity, and save our souls, Gracious One!

Kontakion 11

All the authority in heaven and on earth has been given to our Saviour Who has taught us to obey in everything He had commanded us. Not wanting to leave us orphans, but wishing to be with us forever, He said: And surely I am with you always, to the very end of the ages. After that, ascending into heaven and being seated at the right hand of the Father, He received the Father's promise and send Thee, the Most Holy Spirit, the One Who comes personally but doesn't reveal His person at all. For these, through You we sing: Alleluia!

Oikos 11

Once, at the Last Supper, Saviour Jesus took bread in His sacred, pure and spotless hands and giving thanks He blessed and sanctified it, broke it and gave it to His holy disciples and Apostles, saying: *"Take, eat it: this is my Body"*, then the same manner He also took the cup, when He had

---

[18] *Rev.* 4.13.
[19] *Rev.* 22.17.

supped, saying, *Drink ye all of it; this is my Blood of the new testament, which is shed for you and for many for the remission of sins, do this in remembrance of me,*[20] so He established the Mystery of the Eucharist. Because of that, we say like these:

Come, O Most Holy Spirit, through Whom priests serve the liturgy,

Come, O Most Holy Spirit, by Whom we remember our Lord and God and Savior Jesus Christ,

Come, O Most Holy Spirit, through Whom He surrenders like a lamb to the slaughter,

Come, O Most Holy Spirit, by Whom He is silent as a sheep before its shearers, so He does not open his mouth,

Come, O Most Holy Spirit, by Whom the priests kill the lamb of God, the One Who takes away the sin of the world, for the salvation and the life of the world,

Come, O Most Holy Spirit, by Whom the priests of the Church gore the Lamb's side with a spear and blood and water come out immediately,

Come, O Heavenly King, Comforter, and dwell in us and cleanse us from every impurity, and save our souls, Gracious One!

Kontakion 12

Any song brought to You can not reflect the

---

[20] *Luke* 22.19.

thanksgiving and doxology due to You, Who were from eternity and are and will be forever, having no begining nor end, the One Who is united forever with the Father and with the Son and together accounted, Life and Life-giver, Light and Light-giver, the Good and Source of goodness, by Whom the Father makes Himself known and the Son glorifies and everybody get to know Him, for that we worship the Holy Trinity through You, singing: Alleluia![21]

Oikos 12

All the prophets and divine Apostles, together with the martyrs were crowned through You, amazing hearing, unusual sight. Thee, Who are the Light and Life and living Source, understood with the mind, good, righteous, sympathetic, sovereign, the cleaner of sins, God and deifying, fire from fire proceeding, eloquent, diligent, gift assigner, we call and pray You:

Come, O Most Holy Spirit, the Purple of the Great God, our King,

Come, O Most Holy Spirit, the crystalline and full of jewels Girdle,

Come, O Most Holy Spirit, the unapproachable Sandal,

Come, O Most Holy Spirit, the imperial Coat and the truly sovereign right hand,

Come, O Most Holy Spirit, the One that my villain soul always wished and wants, the One Who made Himself desire in me and made me want to

---

[21]See *Molitfelnic*, Ed. I.B.M.B.O.R., Bucureşti, 2002, p. 700.

sigh after You, the One Who is totally unapproachable,

Come, O Most Holy Spirit, the single One at the single one, because I am lonely as You see, You Who broke me up from all, You changed myself into a solitary on earth,

Come, O Heavenly King, Comforter, and dwell in us and cleanse us from every impurity, and save our souls, Gracious One!

Kontakion 13

(this kontakion should be said three times)

Oh, Heavenly Emperor, the good Comforter, the Spirit of Truth, Who proceed from the Father before the ages and forever rest in the Son, the Unbiased, the Source of the divine gifts, which You share by Your will, through Whom we, the unworthy humans, also were sanctified and chrismated in the day of our baptism, bring us the gift and the power from the height of Thy holy place so that, getting over all desires of the flesh, we live in honesty and purity till the end of our lives, always praising God through You and singing: Alleluia![22]

Then say again Oikos 1 and Kontakion 1.
Then make the end.
Then say this prayer:

---

[22]See *Acatistier*, Ed. Arhiepiscopiei Sucevei si Rădăuţilor, p. 57, 54.

Prayer to the Holy Spirit:

O Heavenly King, Comforter, Who always are as Mystery over all and dwell in the chosen Faces in countless virtues and reveal Yourself and make Yourself a source of perpetual holiness, come and dwell deep within us and purify us, making us worthy of receiving the Holy Trinity; You, Who bestowed us gifts at the very time of our conception, and, as God, You know how it works and how appropriate it is for us, You, through Whom we have life and the growth of life, You, Who came across the holy disciples and Apostles in the third hour, come to us, O Good, and save our souls, guide us throughout the mystery of running towards Christ, open the spiritual sight and the understanding from above, for us to be able to bear spiritual fruits and to acquire the image from Thy outpouring, O Good, making ourselves homes for Christ, entirely in spiritual sweet odor.[23]

---

[23]See Ieromonah Ghelasie Gheorghe și monahul Valerian Dragoș Pâslaru, *Acatistier Sfinții Români*, Ed. Platytera, București, 2013, p. 154-155.

BIBLIOGRAPHY

1. *Acatistier*, Ed. Arhiepiscopiei Sucevei si Rădăuţilor.
2. Diac. Ioan I. Ică jr., *SFÂNTUL SIMEON NOUL TEOLOG Imne, epistole şi capitole Scrieri III*, Ed. Deisis, Sibiu, 2001.
3. *Molitfelnic*, Ed. I.B.M.B.O.R., Bucureşti, 2002.
4. Pr. Prof. Dr. D. Stăniloaie, *Rugăciunea lui Iisus şi experienţa Duhului Sfânt*, Ed. Deisis, Sibiu, 2003.
5. Ieromonah Ghelasie Gheorghe şi monahul Valerian Dragoş Pâslaru, *Acatistier Sfinţii Români*, Ed. Platytera, Bucureşti, 2013.
6. Vladimir Lossky, *Teologia mistică a Bisericii de Răsărit*, Ed. Anastasia, Bucureşti, 1990.

9 786063 012013